HOUSTON
OILERS

STEVE POTTS

CREATIVE ☙ EDUCATION INC.

Published by Creative Education, Inc.
123 S. Broad Street, Mankato, Minnesota 56001

Designed by Rita Marshall

Cover illustration by Lance Hidy Associates

Photos by Allsport, Bettmann Archives, Duomo, Photos
by Sissac, Sportschrome and Wide World Photos

Library of Congress Cataloging-in-Publication Data

Potts, Steve.
    Houston Oilers/Steve Potts.
    p.   cm.
    ISBN 0-88682-368-4
    1. Houston Oilers (Football team)—History.   I. Title.
GV956.H68P68   1990
796.332′64′097561411—dc20   90-41257
                                                 CIP

Television and movies have given us an image of Texas as a "big" state: big cowboy hats, big ranches, big cars. One of the state's other big attractions is pro football, and no team is "bigger" than the Houston Oilers.

However, it hasn't always been that way. In August 1959 Texas millionaires Lamar Hunt and K. S. "Bud" Adams got together with several rich friends and formed the American Football League (AFL). Its competition, the National Football League, had been around since 1922, but when Hunt and Adams had asked for an NFL franchise for Texas, they had been told "no." By 1960, when the first AFL season opened, Texas had two teams, one in Dallas and one

One of the first Houston Oilers, Billy Cannon.

Double duty! Billy Cannon led Houston in both rushing and punt returns.

in Houston. The AFL also had clubs located in Boston, Buffalo, New York, Los Angeles, Oakland, and Denver.

Bud Adams formed the Houston Oilers' in 1959 and has continued as the team's owner and president for over thirty years. One of the sport's biggest boosters, Adams came to love football at an early age. He won football, basketball, and baseball letters at Culver Military Academy, then lettered in football at both Menlo College and the University of Kansas. World War II and success in the oil business ended Adams's hopes for a pro career, but he never lost his love for the pigskin and the gridiron.

Adams translated this love into a never ending quest to provide his team with everything it needed to be successful. One of his biggest achievements in this regard, was his role in getting the $18 million bond issue passed in January 1961 that built the Harris County Domed Stadium, better known as the Houston Astrodome. Sometimes called a "wonder of the modern world," the stadium features AstroTurf, man-made turf created just for the Astrodome.

IMMEDIATE SUCCESS FOR HOUSTON

The Houston Oilers, however, didn't always have such luxurious accommodations. In fact during their first four years (1960–1964), the Oilers played at Jeppesen Stadium, the local high school field. Despite their small home, the Oilers did well, winning first place in the AFL Eastern Division three consecutive years and the league championship in 1960 and 1961.

The Oilers' success was due in part to the fine players

Current Oilers' running back Allen Pinkett (#20).

1 9 6 1

Lucky Seven! Quarterback George Blanda threw for seven touchdowns in a single game.

coach Lou Rymkus hired, drafted, and persuaded to play for the fledgling team. Three of these players eventually entered Houston's record books.

Billy Cannon, a Heisman Trophy winner from Louisiana State University, was selected by the Oilers in the AFL's first player draft. His future in Houston seemed rosy until the Los Angeles Rams produced a signed document claiming Cannon was committed to them. It seemed the LSU star had signed with both AFL and NFL teams. Both Houston and Los Angeles wanted the running back, so they took the case to court. The judge ruled in June 1961 that Houston had a legal right to its draftee, and a happy Cannon joined the team for its first summer training camp.

From this time forward it was evident to many in the Houston organization that he would be a star. "I remember," said coach Rymkus, "seeing Billy Cannon walk into camp and knowing immediately we had a great player." In his three years with the team Cannon set season records in rushing and kickoff and punt returns. In addition, he led the AFL in rushing with 644 yards in 1960 and 948 yards in 1961.

Another member of the Oilers' 1960 and 1961 championship teams was a four-time league all-star named Jim Norton. A man of many talents, safety-punter Norton holds Oiler team records for career punts (519 with a 42.3 yard average) and career interceptions (45).

But perhaps the team's most valuable asset in its early days was a man who came out of semi-retirement to play for Lou Rymkus. George Blanda had played for the Chicago Bears and Baltimore Colts from 1949 to 1958, then sat out the 1959 season. Lured back onto the playing field by the Oilers, Blanda would resume his remarkable career. By the time of his retirement, fifteen years later, Blanda would set all-time NFL records for most games played (340), most seasons played (an astounding 26), most points scored (2,002), and most points scored after touchdowns (943). An unusual player by anyone's standards, Blanda played a strange combination of positions: quarterback and place-kicker. After playing for Houston for seven seasons, he ended his long career at Oakland (1967–1975).

1 9 6 7

The Oilers became division champs thanks in part to the strong defensive play of Ken Houston.

THE OILERS' ROLLERCOASTER RIDE

Ironically, the Houston Oilers, unlike most expansion teams, had their best records in their early years. The years 1964 to 1980 saw the team, its coaches, and its season records rise and fall in a dizzying rollercoaster ride; during this period the Oilers had eight losing years, seven winning seasons, two seasons ending in .500 records, and seven coaches. Houston's fans never knew what to expect when each new year began.

Why the Oilers performed so unevenly is hard to explain, especially since they had three of football's finest athletes during this period. These were performers who, under better conditions, might have led their teammates to the Super Bowl.

Elvin Bethea joined the Oilers in 1968, after a stunning four years at North Carolina A & T. He continued his standout play in Houston. Bethea played in 135 consecutive games with the Oilers, a club record, until breaking his arm in 1977: Bethea claims other club records as well

Grand theft touchdown! Ken Houston scored four TDs on interceptions during the season.

including, most games played, most seasons played (1968-1983), and most Pro Bowl appearances. A defensive end, Bethea was best known, however, for leading his team in six different seasons in sacking opposing quarterbacks.

While Bethea compiled an admirable record, Ken Houston's achievements with the Oilers are truly remarkable. The talented defender has the distinction of being one of only two Oilers in Pro Football's Hall of Fame in Canton, Ohio. But things didn't start so smoothly for Houston. Although his college team was a three-time national champion, pro recruiters paid little attention to him; Houston was only a ninth-round draft choice. What a bargain. This stunning safety ended up playing fourteen seasons, including six with the Oilers, and accumulated forty-nine career interceptions. Selected an astounding twelve consecutive times—in both the AFL and the NFL—to the Pro Bowl team, Houston still holds the NFL record for career interceptions returned for touchdowns.

The third Oilers' player who ranked among football's finest athletes was quarterback Dan Pastorini, a first-round draft choice from Santa Clara. Dan played for Houston from 1971 to 1979. A showman on and off the field, Pastorini had a strong arm that lofted balls for over fourteen hundred yards in nine consecutive seasons, a consistent performance that few opponents could match.

Despite fine individual performances, the Oilers' fortunes were not reversed until they hired a new coach and got the league's number-one draft pick. The Oilers' new helmsman was football's most colorful coach, O. A. "Bum" Phillips. From 1975 to 1980 this former high school coach led the Oilers to five winning seasons, two divisional crowns, and into two AFL championship games. In addition, his 55-35-0 record is the best in franchise history.

Phillips obviously knew football, but it was his appearance on and off the gridiron that grabbed the public's attention. Just a Texas "good ole boy," he usually wore his trademark ten-gallon Stetson hat, lizard or snakeskin boots, and a plaid Western shirt. No matter what his appearance, it soon became clear Bum meant business. After declaring that a little shakeup would be good for the Oilers, Phillips settled down to rebuilding his team.

Hired just three days before the NFL players' draft began, Phillips began his tenure by selecting linebacker Robert Brazile of Jackson State and Texas A & I running back Dan Hardeman in the first round, and Kansas wide receiver Emmett Edwards in the next round to bolster the Oilers' offense.

Brazile, an All-Pro choice as a rookie and again each year from 1976 to 1982, became known as "Dr. Doom" for his effectiveness on the line. He, Hardeman, and Edwards joined Ken Burrough and Billy Johnson, both wide receivers, to bring the Oilers their first winning season in eight years in 1975.

Burrough, who caught passes for 1,063 yards and scored eight touchdowns, led the team in receptions for seven years. Lining up with Burrough at the other wide-out position was Billy Johnson. Nicknamed "White Shoes," Johnson thrilled fans with his punt and kickoff returns; leading the team in both categories from 1974 to 1977. With the

1 9 7 5

Bum Phillips led the Oilers to a 10-4 record in his first season as head coach.

13

Rookie Earl Campbell was magic as he led the league in rushing with 1450 yards.

help of these new players the team's winning ways drew fans back to the Astrodome; home-game ticket sales leaped by one hundred thousand in 1975.

Despite the Oilers' initial success under Phillips' direction, it wasn't until 1978 that Houston really made its mark. The prize plum that Bum Phillips plucked in the draft that year was the incomparable Earl Campbell. Campbell, the 1977 Heisman Trophy winner at the University of Texas and a first-round draft pick in 1978, had not always planned for a career in football.

"The Tyler Rose," as Campbell came to be called in his college days, had grown up in tiny Tyler, Texas. Attracted to pool, cigarettes, and whiskey, he seemed destined for jail. After he was shot in the leg during a drunken brawl, however, Campbell decided to dedicate his life to football. Thus began one of the game's greatest success stories.

Campbell's high school and college records only hinted at what his career in the pros would be like. Through seven seasons and dozens of games, the young running back in jersey number 34, a "gusher of a rusher," turned in one awe-inspiring performance after another. By the time he left the Oilers in 1984, Campbell held virtually all of the club's rushing records and had been named to five Pro Bowls. Today, Campbell still ranks as the NFL's seventh leading rusher, and is eighth in rushing touchdowns.

With his powerful presence, Campbell and company grabbed two division championships in 1978 and 1979, but even more important, they put their team back in the winner's circle. Under the leadership of Bum Phillips, the Oilers posted winning seasons in 1975, 1977, 1978, 1979, and 1980—an impressive record for a team coming off seven consecutive losing seasons.

Campbell and a tough defense led to success.

THE OILERS REBUILD

1 9 8 0

Billy Johnson finished his Houston career ranking tenth on the team's all-time reception list.

In his final year with the Oilers, Bum Phillips was a man possessed. He wanted to win it all. His chance at the Super Bowl had been blocked twice previously by the Pittsburgh Steelers. As he began the 1980 season, Phillips was determined to leap that last hurdle and win a Super Bowl ring.

A controversial trade before the season opener sent Oilers' quarterback Dan Pastorini to Oakland for quarterback Ken Stabler. Pastorini, one of the team's most consistent performers, seemed to be at the height of his career. Stabler, on the other hand, was aging. Could Stabler, known as "The Snake," still captain a winning team?

Stabler's critics rested their wagging tongues as the season unfolded. The Oilers repeated their 1979 record of 11-5 again in 1980. They couldn't, however, get past their playoff jinx. In a sad homecoming for Stabler, the Raiders trounced the Oilers 27-7. Besides losing the game, the Oilers also lost their coach. In a post-game press conference, Phillips had attempted to explain the Oilers' third straight post-season defeat by claiming that Houston, simply enough, was "outplayed and outcoached." While this may have been an honest and accurate judgment, team owner Bud Adams saw Phillips as a defeatist. Furious at the coach's remarks, Adams dismissed him on December 11, 1980. The fired coach had led his team to five straight winning seasons.

Letting Phillips go was one of the club's worst decisions. In the next four seasons Houston went through three coaches, and, in its worst year, sank to a 2-14 record. The face of the team was changing. The offense was decimated

The powerful Earl Campbell. (page 17)

Talented wide receiver Drew Hill, (pages 18–19).

*Houston's fortunes
began to decline
and wouldn't
change until new
stars like Jamie
Williams arrived
several years later.*

by Stabler's departure in 1981 and Earl Campbell's in-
creasingly weak knees. The team could hardly mount a
passing attack or a running game, and the appearance of
three new coaches in four losing seasons signaled that a
Texas-size change was in order.

Houston's reprieve came near the end of the 1985 season, when Oilers' assistant coach Jerry Glanville was ele-
vated to the head position. Glanville, excited at the
prospect of using his big-play philosophy, set his sights on
returning Houston to the playoffs. There was, however,
much to be done. As Glanville graphically stated in an
interview, "When I came here in '84, we had the nicest
guys in the NFL. Their mamas loved 'em. Their daddies
loved 'em. But they wouldn't hit if you handed them
sticks." Glanville was determined to change that. He

wanted to turn the Astrodome into a "House of Pain," a place where visiting teams would feel the power of the Oilers' effective offense and the force of their crushing defense.

Glanville came to Houston with a resumé that made him appear to be the perfect coach to turn the hapless Oilers around. He had been a coach nearly all his adult life. After playing as a linebacker for the Northern Michigan Wildcats in college, Glanville coached in Ohio high schools until 1966. The next year he served as assistant coach at Western Kentucky, where he also received his master's degree. Following that job he joined Georgia Tech's Yellow Jackets in 1968 as an assistant coach. In addition, Glanville's pro coaching background included stints as an assistant with the Detroit Lions, Atlanta Falcons, and Buffalo Bills.

The transition from assistant to head coach, especially head coach of a losing team, is often rough. Glanville's task, however, was made much easier because Hugh Campbell, the coach Glanville replaced, and general manager Ladd Herzeg had been actively recruiting some new young talent to plug the gaps in both the Oilers' defense and offense.

1 9 8 3

The Oilers retired Elvin Bethea's jersey, after Bethea's sixteen years of outstanding defensive play.

A FINE COLLECTION OF TALENT

For three straight years (1982–1984), Houston's staff had worked hard to select offensive linemen to shore up the Oilers' front ranks. The 1982 draft brought Penn State All-American Mike Munchak to Houston as an offensive guard. A frequent choice for the Pro Bowl, Munchak has been hailed as one of the NFL's most effective offensive

Lorenzo White shined behind the blocking of Matthews and Steinkuhler.

linemen. Quarterback sacks allowed have been reduced by 50 percent since Munchak and fellow guard Bruce Matthews teamed up on the offensive line.

Matthews himself, won All-American honors as a senior guard at the University of Southern California. A number-one draft pick in 1983, he has started at all five offensive line positions as a pro. As one sportswriter said, "This guy can do just about anything." Once Matthews settled into the position of right guard in 1988, he had an outstanding record, including a Pro Bowl spot. He and his brother Clay, a Cleveland Browns' linebacker, set an NFL record: for the first time, two brothers were named to play in the same Pro Bowl. Athletic ability just seemed to run in the family, their father, Clay Sr., had also played pro football, as a linebacker for the San Francisco 49ers during the early 1950s.

In a season that saw only three victories, Mike Munchak made his first Pro Bowl appearance.

Houston's first-round draft pick in 1984 was Dean Steinkuhler, one of the NFL's toughest tackles at 6'3" and 280 pounds. Plagued with injuries, Steinkuhler saw little action in 1984 and 1985, but his recent performance led coach Glanville to praise his "inner competitive spirit and his tenacity." Along with teammates Matthews and Munchak, Steinkuhler is part of a crushing, effective offensive line.

At the same time as strengthening the line, Houston's coaches also acted to shore up the team's running and receiving game. Wide receivers Drew Hill and Ernest Givins joined the team and fired up the young Oilers. Hill, who came to the Oilers from the Los Angeles Rams in a 1985 trade, had several fine seasons for Houston. A strong league contender for receiving yards, receptions, and touchdown catches, he ranked first in club receiving yards

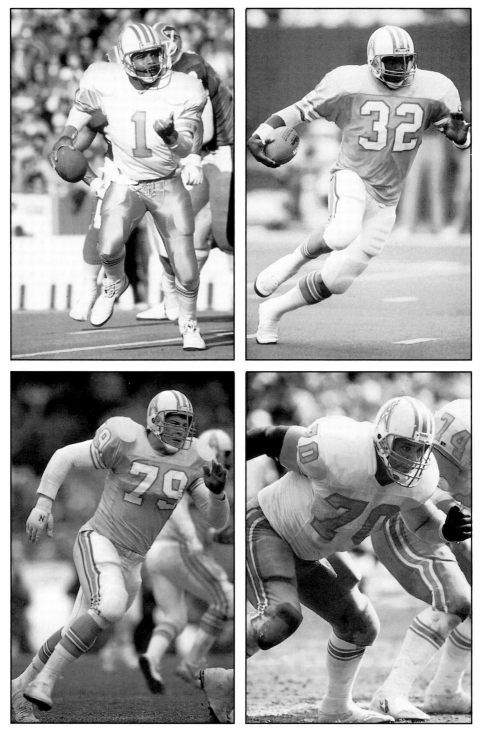

Clockwise: Warren Moon, Alonzo Highsmith, Dean Steinkuhler, Ray Childress.

in 1988. Together, Hill and Givins combined for the most receiving yards for any wide receiver duo in the NFL in both 1987 and 1988.

In college Ernest Givens did it all. He played the positions of receiver, rusher, passer, kick returner, and punt returner as a standout at Louisville. After a fantastic rookie season in 1986—achieving one of the NFL's few one-thousand-yard seasons for pass receptions—Givins earned a reputation as one of pro football's best "after-the-catch" receivers.

1 9 8 8

Watch out defense! Running back Mike Rozier rushed for over a thousand yards during the season.

The Oilers' careful attention to the college and supplemental drafts also won them three of the sport's best running backs: Mike Rozier, Lorenzo White, and Alonzo Highsmith. Describing 1983 Heisman Trophy winner Mike Rozier, coach Glanville said, "I doubt that there's any running back any tougher or more hard-nosed—he may be the toughest guy with a ball under his arm in the whole NFL." Glanville wasn't kidding. After a college career at Nebraska that ended with six Big Eight rushing records, Rozier played in 1984 and the 1985 spring season with two USFL teams. Acquired by Houston in the 1985 supplemental draft, Rozier quickly began producing for the Oilers. In his first four years at Houston, he led the club in rushing, moving him into third place on the Oilers' all-time rushing list.

Rozier's teammate Lorenzo White, was Houston's first-round draft choice in 1988. Although his playing time was limited, he showed the same promise as a rookie that he had as an All-American at Michigan State. A contender for the Heisman Trophy as a sophomore and a senior, White joined Mike Rozier on a team that compiled one of the NFL's best rushing records.

Defensive tackle Ray Childress led a Houston defense that many considered the toughest in the NFL.

The third member of the successful trio was fullback Alonzo Highsmith. Praised as a player who could do "everything—run, catch, block," Highsmith was third in team rushing in 1988. A college standout, Highsmith had followed his father, an offensive lineman in both the NFL and the Canadian Football League (CFL), into football.

The young Houston team and its exciting players were best represented, however, by Oilers' quarterback Warren Moon. Moon followed Hugh Campbell, coach of the Edmonton Eskimos in the Canadian Football League, to Houston as a free agent in 1984. Called the "best quarterback in football" by coach Glanville, Moon played six seasons for Edmonton. During the 1982 and 1983 CFL seasons he passed for an amazing five thousand or more yards and scored over thirty touchdowns both years.

Warren Moon handing off to Alonzo Highsmith.

Defensive co-captain Robert Lyles.

Linebacker John Grimsley.

1 9 9 0

*Rifle-armed
quarterback Warren
Moon directed the
Oilers' new run-
and-shoot offense
into the playoffs.*

In his first five years at Houston, Moon continued his fine play. He started in every game and passed for over fourteen thousand yards and seventy-eight touchdowns. Even after fracturing his shoulder blade early in 1988, he returned to have his best season to date, racking up an impressive 88 percent pass efficiency rating, something most quarterbacks only dream about. When Moon threw the ball, it got to where he wanted it to go.

Despite all this talent, the Oilers had difficulty making it translate into success on the field. Although Glanville accomplished his goal of returning Houston to the playoffs, it wasn't enough. Both 1988 and 1989 saw Glanville's squad make an early exit from the playoffs. Management and fans alike expected more from the Oilers. The result, as usual, was the departure of the head coach.

What lies ahead for the Oilers in the nineties? New coach Jack Pardee, lured away from the University of Houston to replace Jerry Glanville, compiled an impressive 22-11-1 record in his three years at the university. If he can duplicate his previous success, the Oilers have a shot at the Super Bowl. Houston has one of the finest collections of talent in the NFL and is coming off its third successive winning season. For Bud Adams's team, there's nowhere to go but forward. The man that helped to bring pro football to Texas hopes to soon enjoy the sweet taste of victory in football's biggest contest.